CLARINET
REVISED EDITION

J253	Book	6.50
J254	Compact Disc	10.00
J255	Book & CD	16.50

Jump Right In
the instrumental series

Richard F. Grunow
Professor of Music Education
Eastman School of Music
of the University of Rochester

Edwin E. Gordon
Research Professor
University of South Carolina

Christopher D. Azzara
Associate Professor of Music Education
Eastman School of Music
of the University of Rochester

STUDENT BOOK ONE

AN INSTRUMENTAL METHOD DESIGNED FOR DEVELOPING AUDIATION SKILLS AND EXECUTIVE SKILLS

INSTRUMENT	Bk 1	CD 1	Bk1 & CD	Bk 2	CD 2	Bk2 & CD	Solo Bk 1A w. CD	Solo Bk 1B w. CD	Solo Bk 2	Solo Bk 3
Flute	J250	J251	J252	J289		J290	J339	J353	J150	J204
Clarinet	J253	J254	J255	J291		J292	J340	J354	J151	J205
Oboe	J256	J257	J258	J293		J294	J341	J355	J152	J206
Bassoon	J259	J260	J261	J295		J296	J342	J356	J153	J207
Alto Sax	J262	J263	J264	J297		J298	J343	J357	J154	J208
Tenor Sax	J265	J266	J267	J299		J300	J344	J358	J155	J209
Trumpet	J268	J269	J270	J301	J316	J302	J345	J359	J156	J210
Horn in F	J271	J272	J273	J303		J304	J346	J360	J157	J211
Trombone	J274	J275	J276	J305		J306	J347	J361	J158	J212
Baritone BC	J277	J278	J279	J307		J308	J348	J362	J159	J213
Baritone TC	J280	J281	J282	J309		J310	J349	J363	J160	J214
Tuba	J283	J284	J285	J311		J312	J350	J364	J161	J215
Percussion	J286	J287	J288	J313		J314	J351	J365	J162	J216
Recorder	J231	J232	J233	J247	J245CD	J245	J94		J149	J217

Revised Teacher Guide for Band Books 1 and 2 .... J315
Solo Book 1–Writing (all instruments) J167
Solo Book 2–Writing (all instruments) J168
Solo Book 3–Writing (all instruments) J203
Composition Book 1 (all instruments) J249
Revised Teacher's Guide for Recorder J235
GIA Heavy Duty Sporano Recorder M447
JRI for Strings (specify instrument)

CONCERT SELECTIONS
Full score (all twelve works) J178
Flute (J179) • Oboe (J180) • Clarinet I (J181) • Clarinet II (J182) • Bass Clarinet (J183) • Bassoon (J184) • Alto Saxophone (J185) • Tenor Saxophone (J186) • Baritone Saxophone (J187) • Trumpet I (J188) • Trumpet II (J189) • Horn (J190) • Trombone I (J191) • Trombone II (J192) • Baritone B.C. (J193) • Baritone T.C. (J194) • Tuba (J195) • Bells/Xylophone/Piano (J196) • Percussion (J197)
Demonstration compact disc J198CD

RECORDED SOLOS WITH ACCOMPANIMENTS

Cassette Bk 1A & 1B :	Cassette Bk 2:	Cassette Bk 3:
J99	J148	J200
CD Bk 1:	CD Bk 2:	CD Bk 3:
J99CD	J148CD	J200CD

LISTENING

Simple Gifts	Don Gato	You Are My Sunshine
Cassette:	Cassette:	Cassette:
J229CS	J201CS	J199CS
CD:	CD:	CD:
J229CD	J201CD	J199CD

GIA Publications, Inc., 7404 S. Mason Ave., Chicago, IL 60638

ASSIGNMENT SCHEDULE

The teacher will specify the student's assignments. The student will insert the date and check (✓) underneath the date to indicate specific assignments. The *Home-Study Compact Disc* Track # is the same as the Item Number.

READ THE FOLLOWING	Page No.
A NOTE TO PARENTS AND STUDENTS	ii
PRACTICE TIPS	4
USE OF THE *HOME-STUDY COMPACT DISC*	5
PLAYING IN TUNE WITH THE *HOME-STUDY COMPACT DISC*	5
FORMING THE EMBOUCHURE	6
PERFORMING ON THE MOUTHPIECE AND BARREL ASSEMBLY	6
RIGHT HAND POSITION - LEFT HAND POSITION	7
POSTURE - INSTRUMENT POSITION	7
MUSICAL ENRICHMENT	47

LISTEN TO THE HOME-STUDY COMPACT DISC AND FOLLOW THE DIRECTIONS FOR

Item/Track No.	Unit
1 - Singing "Major Duple" a-Melody b-Bass Line	1-A
2 - Accompaniment for Singing "Major Duple"	
3 - Connected Style of Articulation	
4 - Separated Style of Articulation	
5 - Singing "Major Triple" a-Melody b-Bass Line	1-B
6 - Accompaniment for Singing "Major Triple"	
7 - Connected and Separated Styles of Articulation with the Airstream	
8 - Connected and Separated Styles of Articulation on the Mouthpiece and Barrel Assembly	
9 - Singing "Minor Duple" a-Melody b-Bass Line	2-A
10 - Accompaniment for Singing "Minor Duple"	
11 - Tonal Patterns - Major - Tonic and Dominant - Neutral Syllable	
12 - Tonal Patterns - Major - Tonic and Dominant - Tonal Syllables	
13 - Connected and Separated Styles of Articulation on C-DO	
14 - Singing "Minor Triple" a-Melody b-Bass Line	2-B
15 - Accompaniment for Singing "Minor Triple"	
16 - Connected and Separated Styles of Articulation on TI	
17 - Melodic Patterns on C-DO and TI	
18 - Rhythm Patterns - Duple - Macro and Micro - Neutral Syllable	
19 - Rhythm Patterns - Duple - Macro and Micro - Rhythm Syllables	
20 - Singing "Pierrot" a-Melody b-Bass Line	3-A
21 - Accompaniment for Singing "Pierrot"	
22 - Tonal Patterns - Minor - Tonic and Dominant - Neutral Syllable	
23 - Tonal Patterns - Minor - Tonic and Dominant - Tonal Syllables	
24 - Connected and Separated Styles of Articulation on RE	
25 - Melodic Patterns on C-DO, TI and RE	

Copyright © 2000 by GIA Publications, Inc. 7404 South Mason Avenue, Chicago, IL 60638
International copyright secured. All rights reserved. Printed in the United States of America

Item/Track No.	DATE	DATE	DATE	DATE	DATE	DATE	DATE	DATE	DATE	DATE	DATE	DATE	DATE	DATE	DATE
26 - Singing "Go Tell Aunt Rhody" a-Melody b-Bass Line 3-B															
27 - Accompaniment for Singing "Go Tell Aunt Rhody"															
28 - Rhythm Patterns - Triple - Macro and Micro - Neutral Syllable															
29 - Rhythm Patterns - Triple - Macro and Micro - Rhythm Syllables															
30 - Connected and Separated Styles of Articulation on MI															
31 - Melodic Patterns on MI and RE															
32 - Melodic Patterns on C-DO, TI, RE and MI															
33 - Patterns from "Major Duple" - Connected Style															
34 - Patterns from "Major Duple" - Separated Style															
35 - Performances of "Major Duple" - Connected and Separated Styles															
36 - "Major Duple" - Accompaniments Only															
37 - Singing "Twinkle, Twinkle, Little Star" a-Melody b-Bass Line 4-A															
38 - Accompaniment for Singing "Twinkle, Twinkle, Little Star"															
39 - Patterns from "Major Triple" - Connected Style															
40 - Patterns from "Major Triple" - Separated Style															
41 - Performances of "Major Triple" - Connected and Separated Styles															
42 - "Major Triple" - Accompaniments Only															
43 - Melodic Patterns on F-DO and TI															
44 - Singing "Hot Cross Buns" a-Melody b-Bass Line 4-B															
45 - Accompaniment for Singing "Hot Cross Buns"															
46 - Melodic Patterns on F-DO, TI, and RE															
47 - Melodic Patterns on MI and RE															
48 - Melodic Patterns on F-DO, TI, RE, and MI															
49 - Patterns from "Pierrot"															
50 - Performance of "Pierrot"															
51 - "Pierrot" - Accompaniment Only															
52 - Singing "Lightly Row" a-Melody b-Bass Line 5-A															
53 - Accompaniment for Singing "Lightly Row"															
54 - Melodic Patterns on D-LA and SI															
55 - Melodic Patterns on D-LA, SI, TI, and DO															
56 - Performances of "Minor Duple" - Connected and Separated Styles															
57 - Performances of "Minor Triple" - Connected and Separated Styles															
58 - "Minor Duple" - Accompaniments Only															
59 - "Minor Triple" - Accompaniments Only															
60 - Singing "Down By the Station" a-Melody b-Bass Line 5-B															
61 - Accompaniment for Singing "Down By the Station"															
62 - Rhythm Patterns - Duple - Divisions - Neutral Syllable															
63 - Rhythm Patterns - Duple - Divisions - Rhythm Syllables															
64 - Melodic Patterns on G-DO and SO															
65 - Melodic Patterns on SO and LA															
66 - Melodic Patterns on G-DO, RE, MI, FA, SO, and LA															
67 - Performance of "Twinkle, Twinkle, Little Star"															
68 - "Twinkle, Twinkle, Little Star" - Accompaniment Only															
69 - "Go Tell Aunt Rhody" - Accompaniment Only (G-DO)															

			DATE	DATE	DATE	DATE	DATE	DATE	DATE	DATE	DATE	DATE	DATE	DATE
70	- Singing "Triple Twinkle" a-Melody b-Bass Line	6-A												
71	- Accompaniment for Singing "Triple Twinkle"													
72	- Tonal Patterns - Major - Tonic, Dominant, Subdominant - Neutral Syllable													
73	- Tonal Patterns - Major - Tonic, Dominant, Subdominant - Tonal Syllables													
74	- Singing "Minor Aunt Rhody" a-Melody b-Bass Line	6-B												
75	- Accompaniment for Singing "Minor Aunt Rhody"													
76	- Rhythm Patterns - Triple - Divisions - Neutral Syllable													
77	- Rhythm Patterns - Triple - Divisions - Rhythm Syllables													
78	- "Lightly Row" - Accompaniment Only (G-DO)													
79	- Singing "Triple Pierrot" a-Melody b-Bass Line	7-A												
80	- Accompaniment for Singing "Triple Pierrot"													
81	- Tonal Patterns - Minor - Tonic, Dominant, Subdominant - Neutral Syllable													
82	- Tonal Patterns - Minor - Tonic, Dominant, Subdominant - Tonal Syllables													
83	- "Down By the Station" - Accompaniment Only (G-DO)													
84	- Singing "Patsy, Ory, Ory, Aye" a-Melody b-Bass Line	7-B												
85	- Accompaniment for Singing "Patsy, Ory, Ory, Aye"													
86	- Rhythm Patterns - Duple - Elongations - Neutral Syllable													
87	- Rhythm Patterns - Duple - Elongations - Rhythm Syllables													
88	- Singing "Baa, Baa, Black Sheep" a-Melody b-Bass Line	8-A												
89	- Accompaniment for Singing "Baa, Baa, Black Sheep"													
90	- Singing "Oats, Peas, Beans" a-Melody b-Bass Line	8-B												
91	- Accompaniment for Singing "Oats, Peas, Beans"													
92	- Rhythm Patterns - Triple - Elongations - Neutral Syllable													
93	- Rhythm Patterns - Triple - Elongations - Rhythm Syllables													
94-97	Musical Enrichment - See page 47.													

PRACTICE TIPS

Under typical circumstances, you should practice every day. When first learning to play an instrument, however, it is most effective if you practice for shorter periods of time. Two sessions of 10 to 15 minutes each day are better than one longer session. Although you will be able to practice for longer periods of time after the first several lessons, it will still be most beneficial if you continue practicing for two shorter sessions, as opposed to one longer session.

How you practice is more important than the length of time you practice. To establish goals for each practice session you should refer to the *Assignment Schedule* on pages 2 - 4, along with the information and illustrations on pages 5 - 7. It is also important to read carefully the guidelines for developing executive skills, which include embouchure, articulation, fingering, posture, and hand position.

USE OF THE HOME-STUDY COMPACT DISC

The *Home-Study Compact Disc* (CD) is an important part of *Jump Right In: The Instrumental Series*. The CD should be played on good equipment. If you do not have a CD player, ask your teacher if you may use one to practice with during the school day, or if you may borrow a CD player from the school or a music store until you obtain your own.

You will use the CD when you practice at home. During your lessons at school, your teacher will explain how to practice at home with your CD. Every item on the CD will be used to help you learn a specific assignment in this book, as explained on the *Assignment Schedule* on pages 2 - 4. For example, after the first lesson you will be asked to listen to the CD and follow the directions for Items 1, 2, 3, and 4. Listen to and follow the directions as many times as you wish. You may replay items on the CD as many times as necessary. Ask your teacher for permission, however, before you listen to items that have not been assigned.

When using the CD, you will typically want to review previous assignments. Perhaps there will be times when you will wish to start with the assignment given in your last lesson. In that case, simply call up the number of that item on the CD player. If you have the "repeat" option on your CD player, you may use it to repeat the item as many times as you wish.

Ask your teacher for help if you are having a problem with following the directions for *Use of the Home-Study Compact Disc*. Protect your CD when you are not practicing by storing it in the plastic sleeve included in this book.

PLAYING IN TUNE WITH THE HOME-STUDY COMPACT DISC

Adjust your clarinet here.

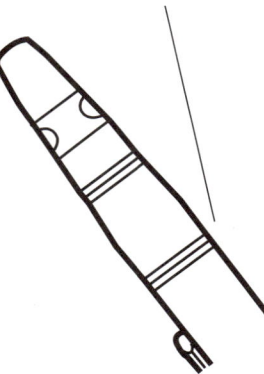

Figure 1.

Because the speed of compact disc players is generally consistent, you will be able to play in tune with the compact disc with just a slight adjustment of the distance between the mouthpiece/barrel assembly and the upper joint of the clarinet. See Figure 1. Remember to twist and turn the mouthpiece and barrel assembly when tuning your instrument. Do not pull on the mouthpiece and barrel assembly. Always keep several reeds available, and keep them in a protective holder. See Figure 2. The quality of reed and mouthpiece and the correct assembly of the reed and mouthpiece are also important factors contributing to good intonation on your clarinet. Ask your teacher to help you when selecting reeds and when assembling the reed and mouthpiece. In addition to performing on your instrument, you will benefit by listening to the compact disc and by singing the songs, chanting the rhythm patterns, and singing the tonal patterns. Except when playing with the accompaniments that are provided on the compact disc, you should ALWAYS REPEAT on your instrument AFTER you hear the musical example on the compact disc. DO NOT PERFORM on your instrument WITH what you are hearing on the compact disc.

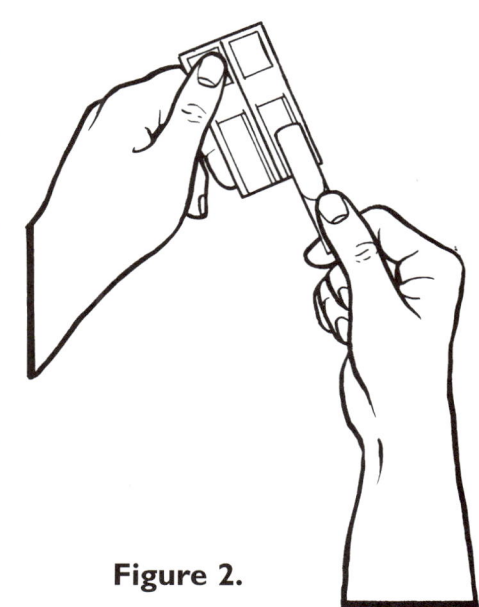

Figure 2.

FORMING THE EMBOUCHURE

The embouchure (pronounced AHM-bu-sher) refers to the position of the lips when making a sound on the clarinet. The establishment of a good embouchure will do much to aid your musical progress in the weeks and years ahead. Follow the steps listed below to form the embouchure and perform on the clarinet mouthpiece and barrel assembly. Check frequently in the mirror to make certain that your embouchure is similar to the one in the picture. Because no two persons have identical physical characteristics, no two clarinet players have identical embouchures.

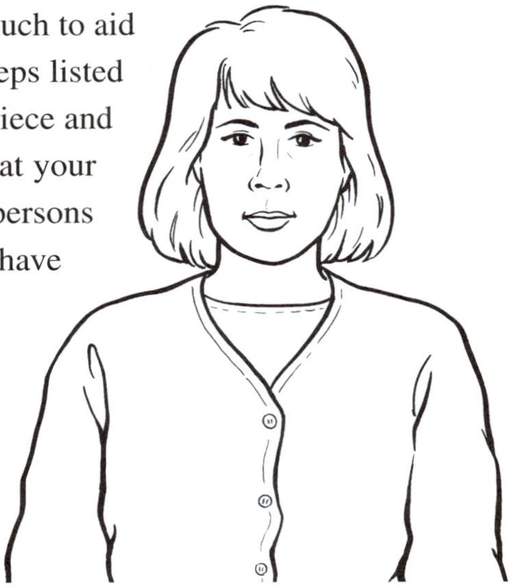

Step 1 - Place the end of the reed in your mouth to soak for 1-2 minutes. Assemble the mouthpiece and barrel following your teacher's instructions.

Step 2 - Place your lips in a position to say "Mmmm." (Your top teeth and bottom teeth should not be touching.) See Figure 3.

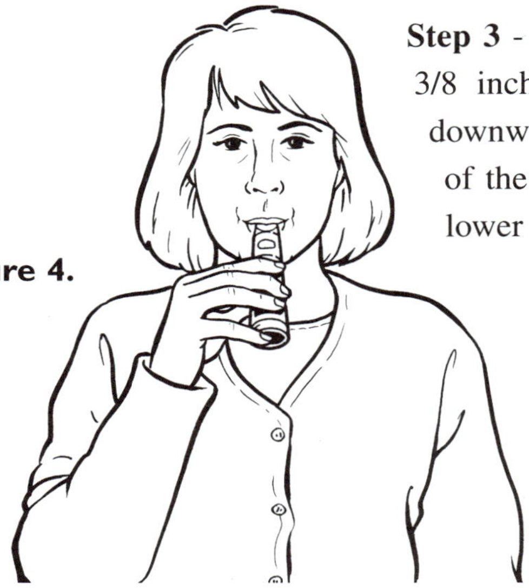

Figure 3.

Step 3 - Open your mouth so that the teeth are approximately 3/8 inch apart. Point the chin and draw the chin muscles downward while covering the lower teeth with the upper part of the lower lip. A concavity should be visible between the lower lip and chin.

Step 4 - Place the mouthpiece in your mouth with the upper teeth touching the mouthpiece approximately 3/8 of an inch from the end. Seal the lips around the mouthpiece creating equal pressure from all directions. See Figure 4.

Figure 4.

PERFORMING ON THE CLARINET MOUTHPIECE AND BARREL ASSEMBLY

Step 1 - Follow Steps 1-4 from above.

Step 2 - Begin blowing a steady stream of air through the mouthpiece and barrel assembly while keeping the corners of the mouth firm. (Firm corners will prevent the cheeks from puffing.) Perform first with the connected style of articulation, "doo, doo, doo, doo," and then with the separated style of articulation, "too, too, too, too." See Figure 5. Listen to Item #8 on the *Home-Study Compact Disc*.

Figure 5.

RIGHT HAND POSITION

Step 1 - Place your right hand to the lower part of the clarinet with your thumb under the thumb rest at the point corresponding to the base of the finger nail. See Figure 6.

Step 2 - Slant your fingers downward slightly while maintaining a natural curve.

Step 3 - Center the fleshy part of your finger tips on the holes or keys while keeping your thumb and wrist straight. See Figures 6-7.

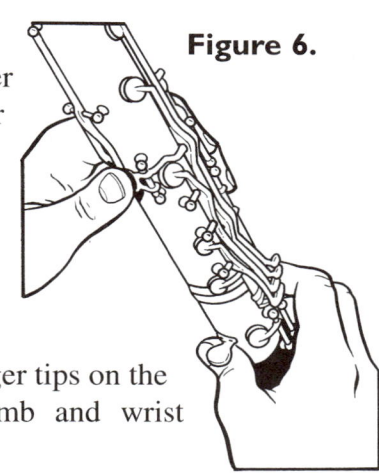

Figure 6.

Figure 7.

LEFT HAND POSITION

Step 1 - Place your left hand to the upper part of the clarinet with your thumb diagonally across the thumb hole. See Figure 8.

Step 2 - Slant your fingers downward slightly while maintaining a natural curve.

Step 3 - Center the fleshy part of your finger tips on the holes or keys while keeping your thumb and wrist straight. See Figures 8-9.

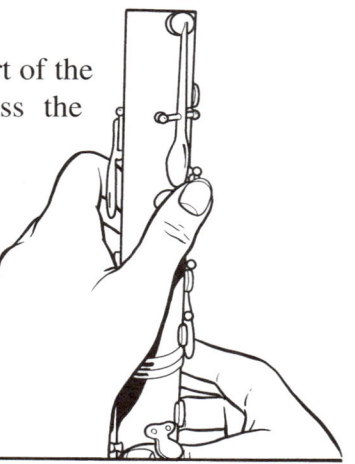

Figure 8.

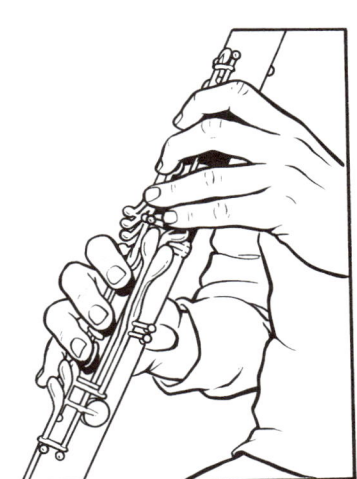

Figure 9.

POSTURE

Step 1 - Stand erect in front of the chair that you are using.

Step 2 - Seat yourself in the chair by bending at your knees but not at your waist.

- The back is straight.
- The shoulders are relaxed.
- The feet are comfortably apart and flat on the floor. See Figure 10.

INSTRUMENT POSITION

- The entire weight of the clarinet is supported by the right thumb.
- The clarinet is held to the center of the body with the bell placed approximately between the knees.
- The elbows are comfortably situated away from the body. See Figure 10.

Figure 10.

CLARINET FINGERINGS

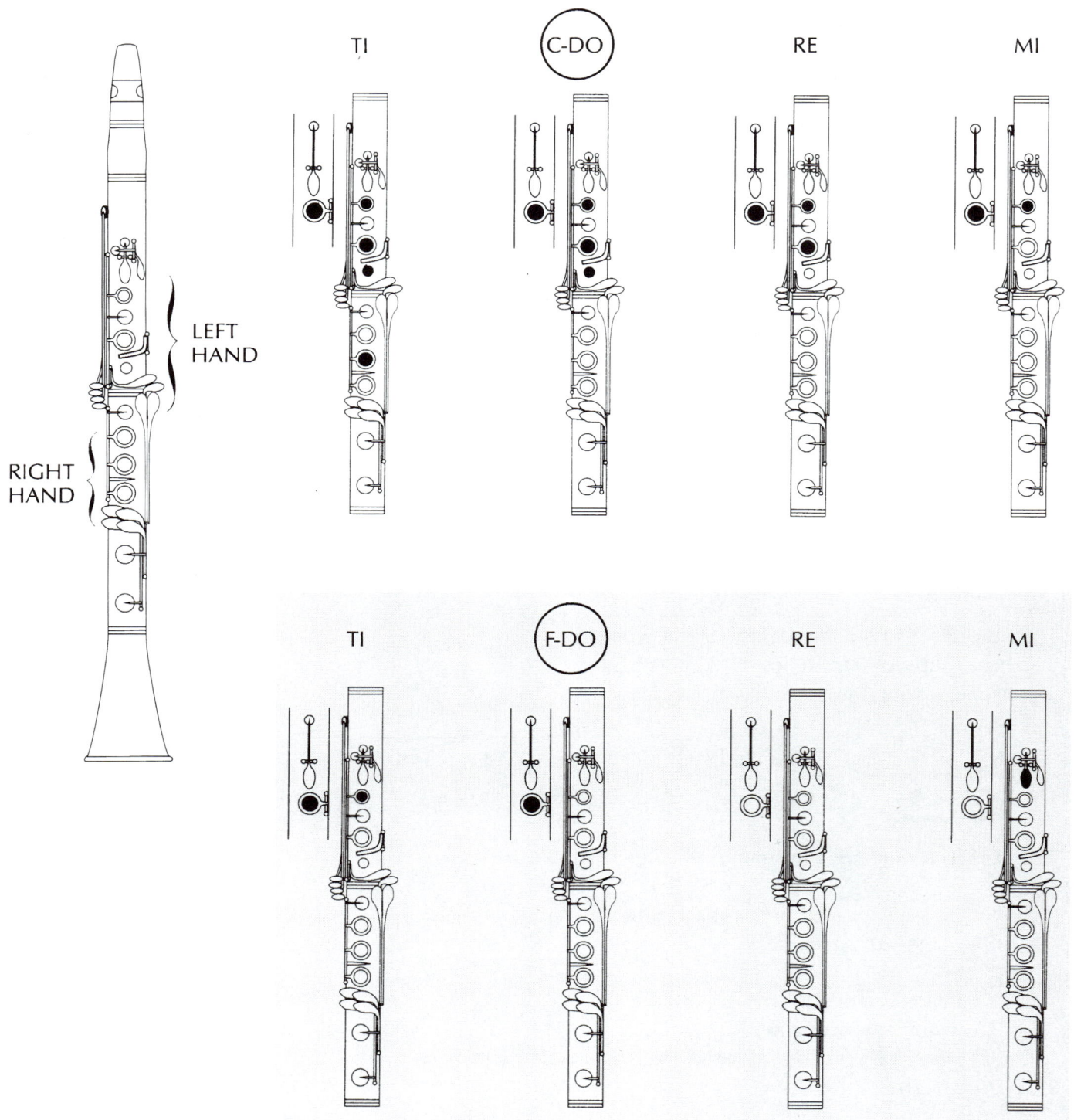

CLARINET FINGERINGS

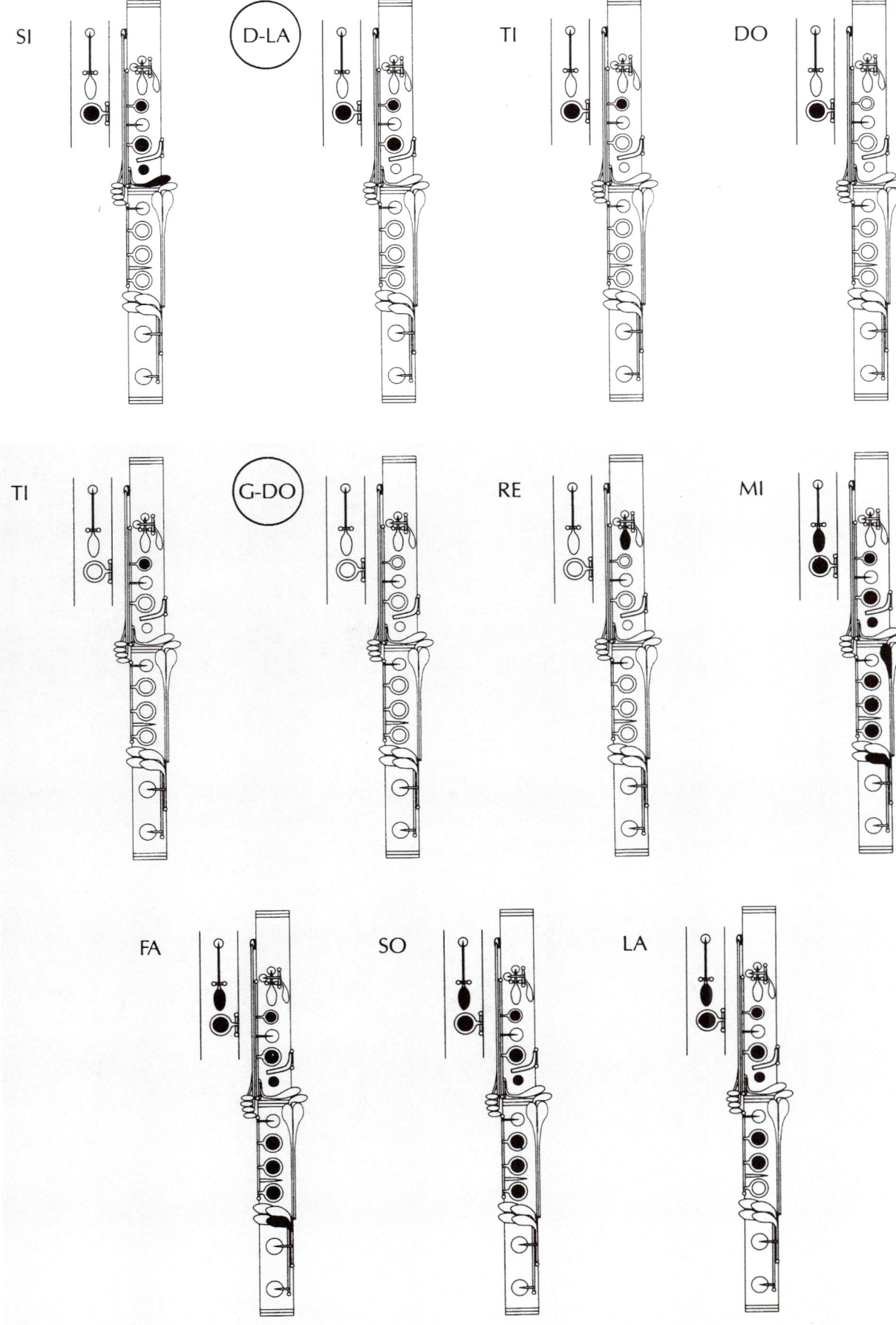

TONAL READING
TONIC AND DOMINANT FUNCTIONS IN C MAJOR

1. Read the following patterns by singing them WITH TONAL SYLLABLES and by performing them on your instrument. The arrow points to DO. C indicates a TONIC pattern in major tonality; G7 indicates a DOMINANT pattern in major tonality.

2. Read the following series of patterns by singing them WITH TONAL SYLLABLES and by performing them on your instrument. The arrow points to DO. C indicates a TONIC pattern in major tonality; G7 indicates a DOMINANT pattern in major tonality.

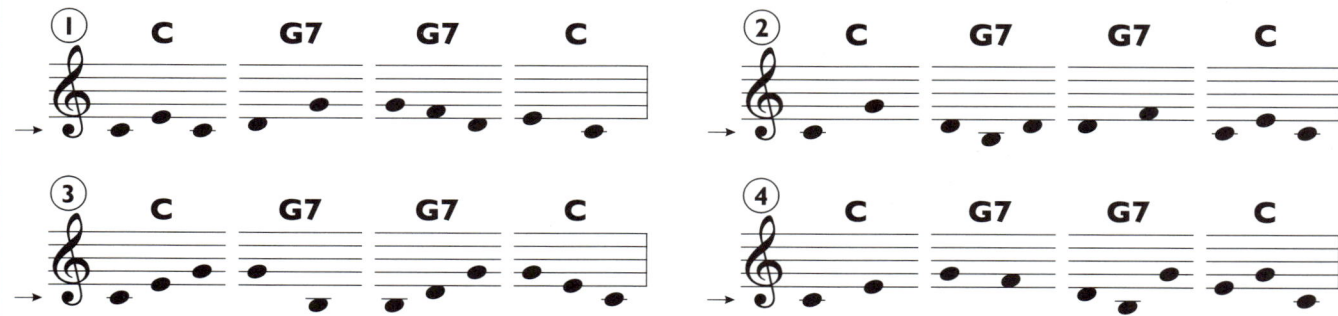

Be expressive when performing with your voice and with your instrument!

RHYTHM READING
MACROBEATS AND MICROBEATS IN DUPLE METER

1. Read the following patterns by chanting them WITH RHYTHM SYLLABLES and by performing them on your instrument.

   The number (2) tells how many macrobeats there are in a measure.
   The symbol (♩) indicates the kind of note that is a macrobeat.

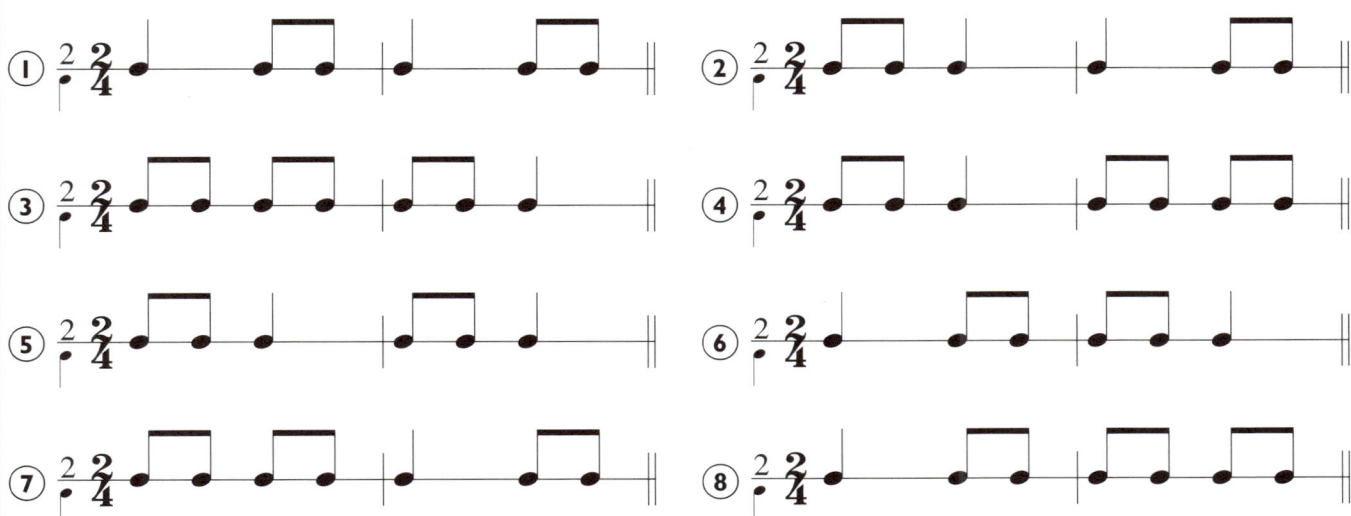

2. Read the following series of patterns by chanting them WITH RHYTHM SYLLABLES and by performing them on your instrument.

   The number (2) tells how many macrobeats there are in a measure.
   The symbol (♩) indicates the kind of note that is a macrobeat.

Be expressive when performing with your voice and with your instrument!

MAJOR DUPLE

RHYTHM READING
MACROBEATS AND MICROBEATS IN TRIPLE METER

1. Read the following patterns by chanting them WITH RHYTHM SYLLABLES and by performing them on your instrument.

    The number (2) tells how many macrobeats there are in a measure.
    The symbol (♩·) indicates the kind of note that is a macrobeat.

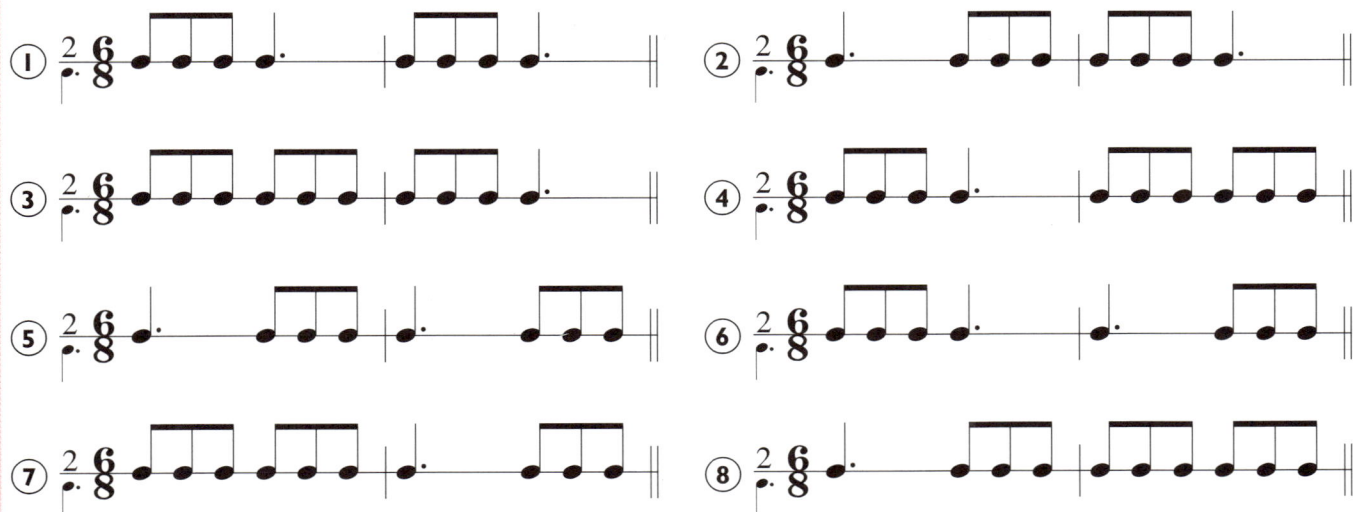

2. Read the following series of patterns by chanting them WITH RHYTHM SYLLABLES and by performing them on your instrument.

    The number (2) tells how many macrobeats there are in a measure.
    The symbol (♩·) indicates the kind of note that is a macrobeat.

Be expressive when performing with your voice and with your instrument!

MAJOR TRIPLE

ENRHYTHMIC READING
MACROBEATS AND MICROBEATS IN DUPLE METER

1. Read the following patterns by chanting them WITH RHYTHM SYLLABLES and by performing them on your instrument. The patterns on the left (4/4) are enrhythmic (they sound the same, but look different) with the patterns on the right (¢).

   The numbers (4, 2) indicate how many macrobeats are in a measure.
   The symbols (♩ , ♩) indicate what kind of a note is a macrobeat.

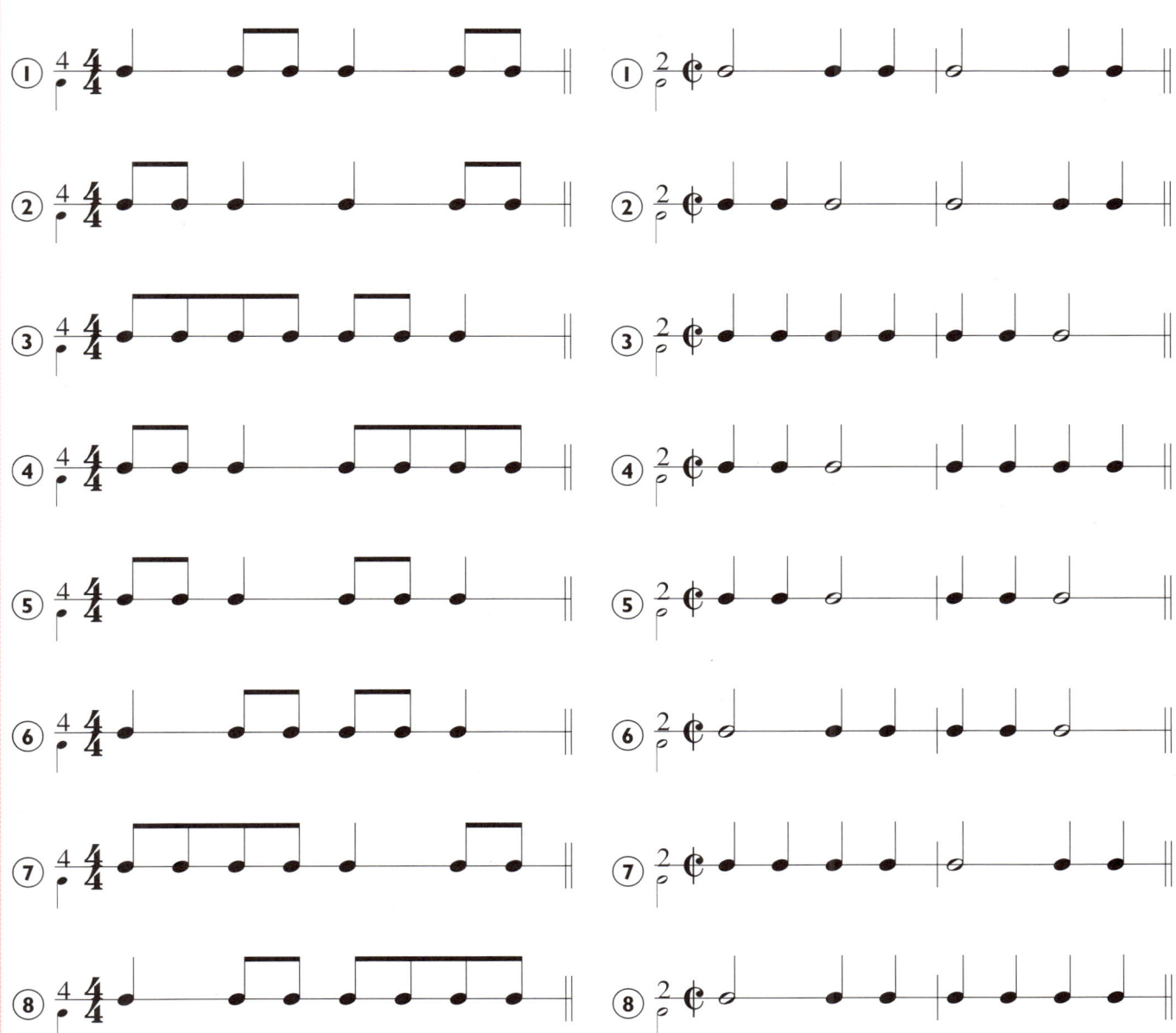

Be expressive when performing with your voice and with your instrument!

MAJOR DUPLE

ENRHYTHMIC READING
MACROBEATS AND MICROBEATS IN TRIPLE METER

1. Read the following patterns by chanting them WITH RHYTHM SYLLABLES and by performing them on your instrument. The patterns on the left (3/8) are enrhythmic (they sound the same, but look different) with the patterns on the right (3/4).

   The numbers (1, 1) indicate how many macrobeats are in a measure.
   The symbols (♩. , ♩.) indicate what kind of a note is a macrobeat.

Be expressive when performing with your voice and with your instrument!

MAJOR TRIPLE

TONAL READING
TONIC AND DOMINANT FUNCTIONS IN F MAJOR

1. Read the following patterns by singing them WITH TONAL SYLLABLES and by performing them on your instrument. The arrow points to DO. F indicates a TONIC pattern in major tonality; C7 indicates a DOMINANT pattern in major tonality.

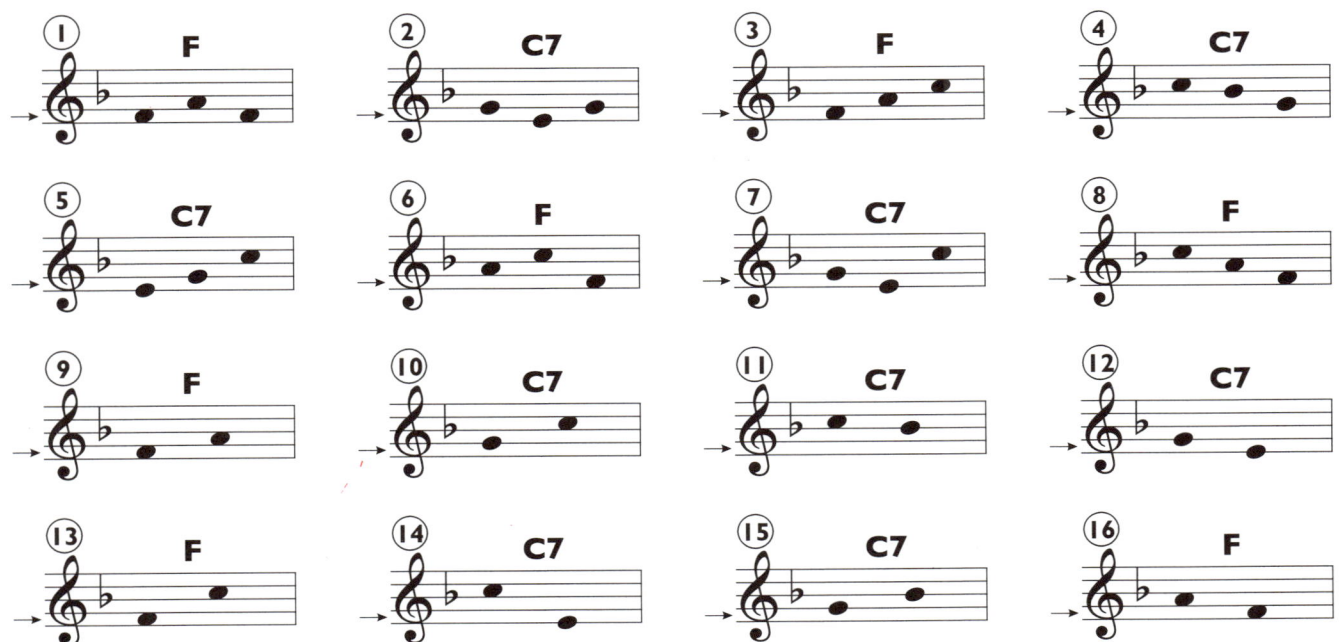

2. Read the following series of patterns by singing them WITH TONAL SYLLABLES and by performing them on your instrument. The arrow points to DO. F indicates a TONIC pattern in major tonality; C7 indicates a DOMINANT pattern in major tonality.

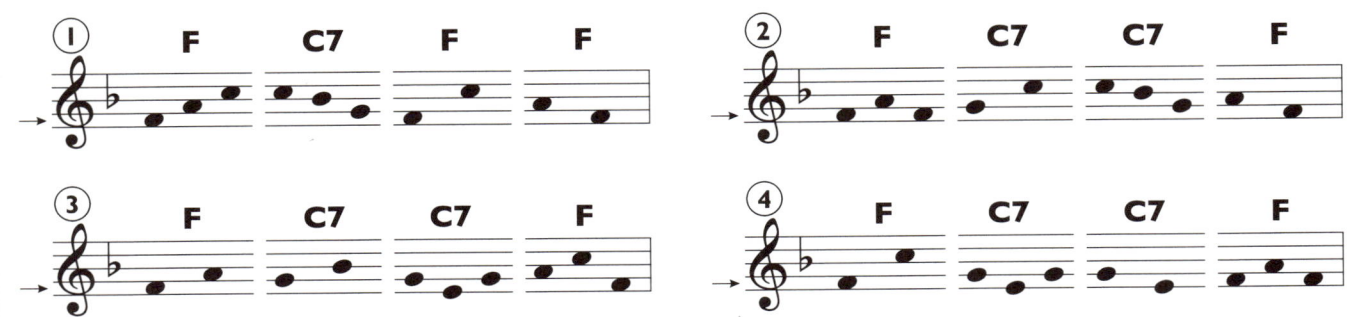

Be expressive when performing with your voice and with your instrument!

TONAL READING
TONIC, DOMINANT, AND SUBDOMINANT FUNCTIONS IN F MAJOR

1. Read the following patterns by singing them WITH TONAL SYLLABLES and by performing them on your instrument. The arrow points to DO. F indicates a TONIC pattern in major tonality; C7 indicates a DOMINANT pattern in major tonality; and B♭ indicates a SUBDOMINANT pattern in major tonality.

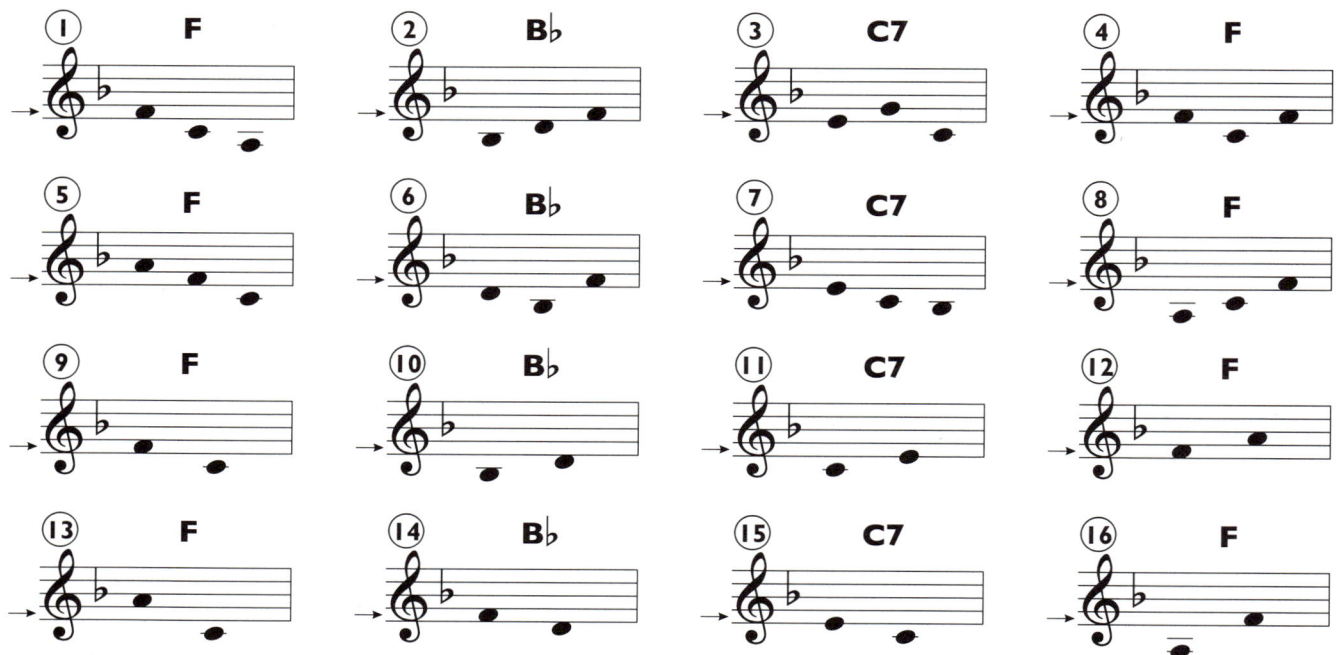

2. Read the following series of patterns by singing them WITH TONAL SYLLABLES and by performing them on your instrument. The arrow points to DO. F indicates a TONIC pattern in major tonality; C7 indicates a DOMINANT pattern in major tonality; and B♭ indicates a SUBDOMINANT pattern in major tonality.

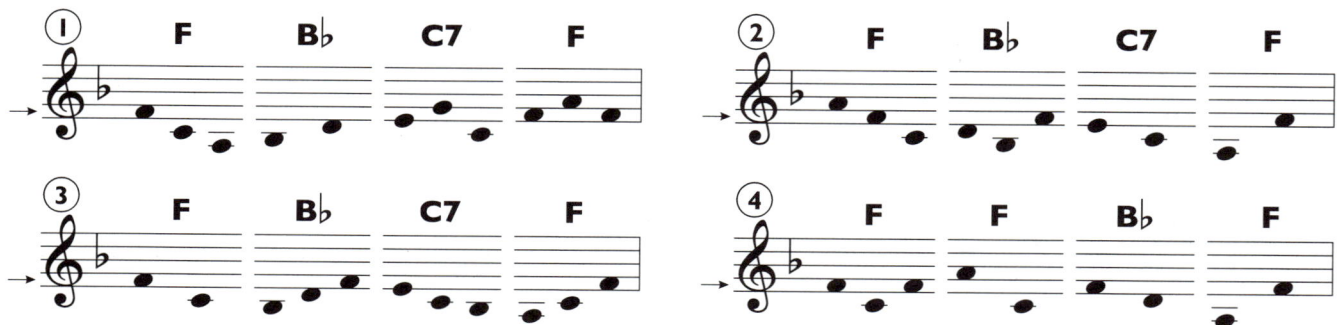

Be expressive when performing with your voice and with your instrument!

TONAL READING
TONIC AND DOMINANT FUNCTIONS IN D MINOR

1. Read the following patterns by singing them WITH TONAL SYLLABLES and by performing them on your instrument. The arrow points to DO. Dm indicates a TONIC pattern in minor tonality; A7 indicates a DOMINANT pattern in minor tonality.

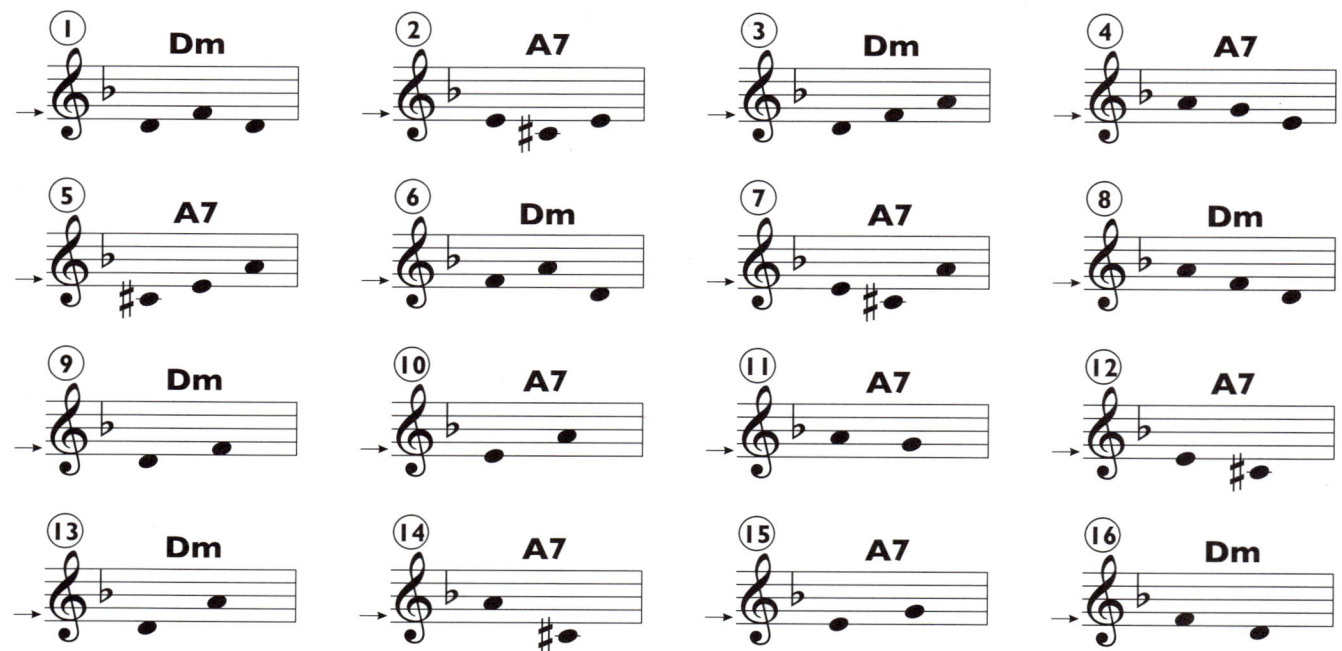

2. Read the following series of patterns by singing them WITH TONAL SYLLABLES and by performing them on your instrument. The arrow points to DO. Dm indicates a TONIC pattern in minor tonality; A7 indicates a DOMINANT pattern in minor tonality.

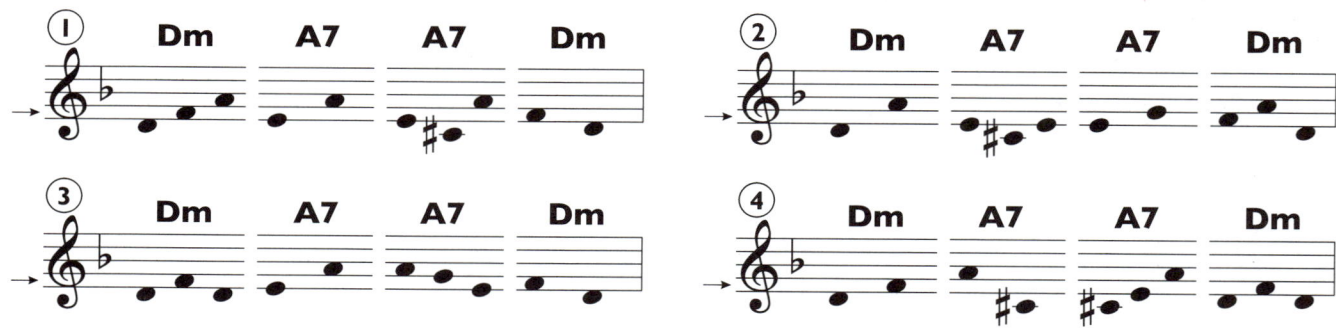

Be expressive when performing with your voice and with your instrument!

MINOR DUPLE

MINOR TRIPLE

RHYTHM READING
MACROBEATS, MICROBEATS, AND DIVISIONS IN DUPLE METER

1. Read the following patterns by chanting them WITH RHYTHM SYLLABLES and by performing them on your instrument.

   The number (2) tells how many macrobeats there are in a measure.
   The symbol (♩) indicates the kind of note that is a macrobeat.

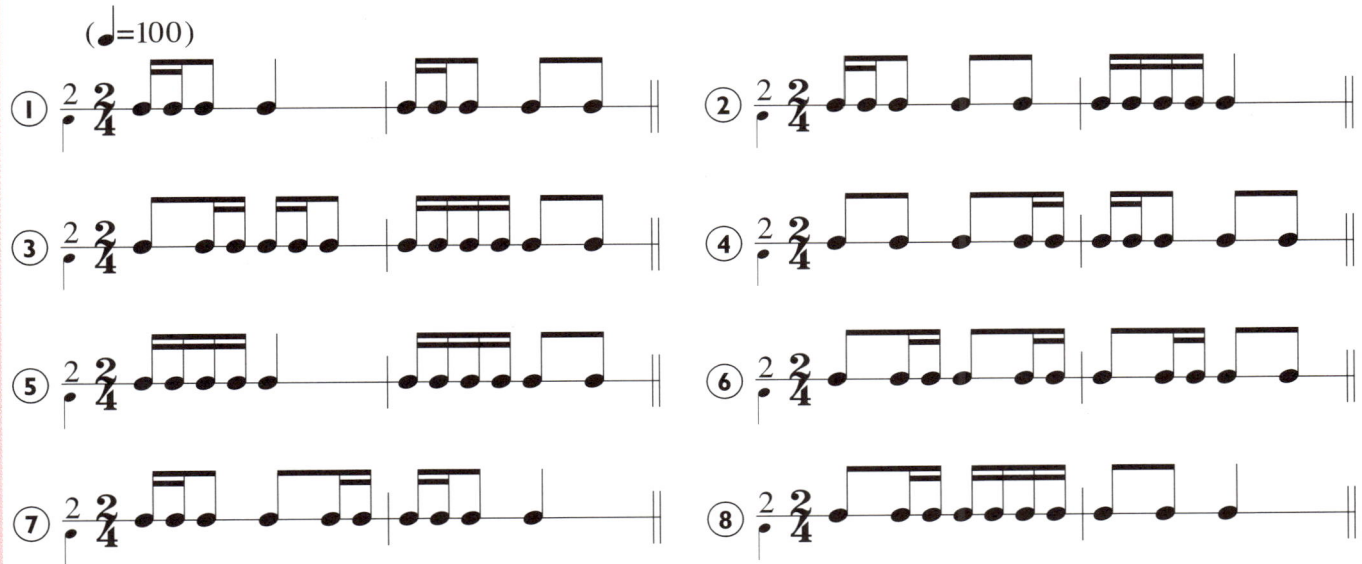

2. Read the following series of patterns by chanting them WITH RHYTHM SYLLABLES and by performing them on your instrument.

   The number (2) tells how many macrobeats there are in a measure.
   The symbol (♩) indicates the kind of note that is a macrobeat.

Be expressive when performing with your voice and with your instrument!

TONAL READING
TONIC AND DOMINANT FUNCTIONS IN G MAJOR

1. Read the following patterns by singing them WITH TONAL SYLLABLES and by performing them on your instrument. The arrow points to DO. G indicates a TONIC pattern in major tonality; D7 indicates a DOMINANT pattern in major tonality.

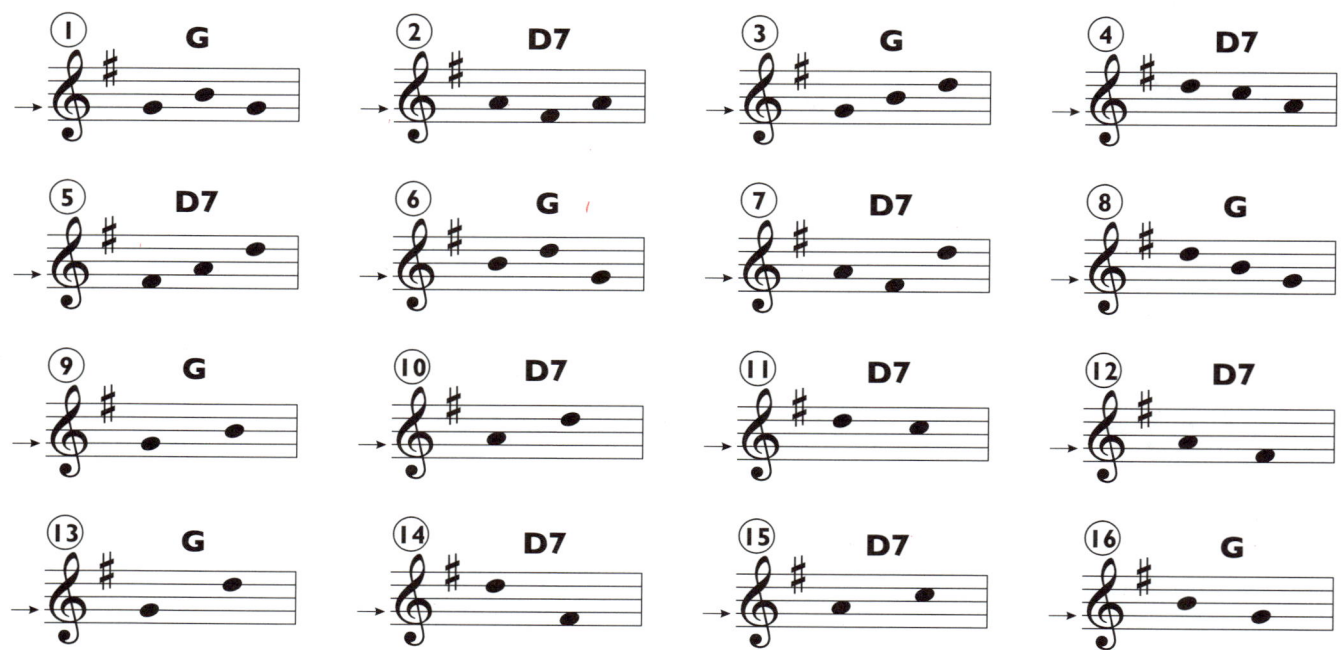

2. Read the following series of patterns by singing them WITH TONAL SYLLABLES and by performing them on your instrument. The arrow points to DO. G indicates a TONIC pattern in major tonality; D7 indicates a DOMINANT pattern in major tonality.

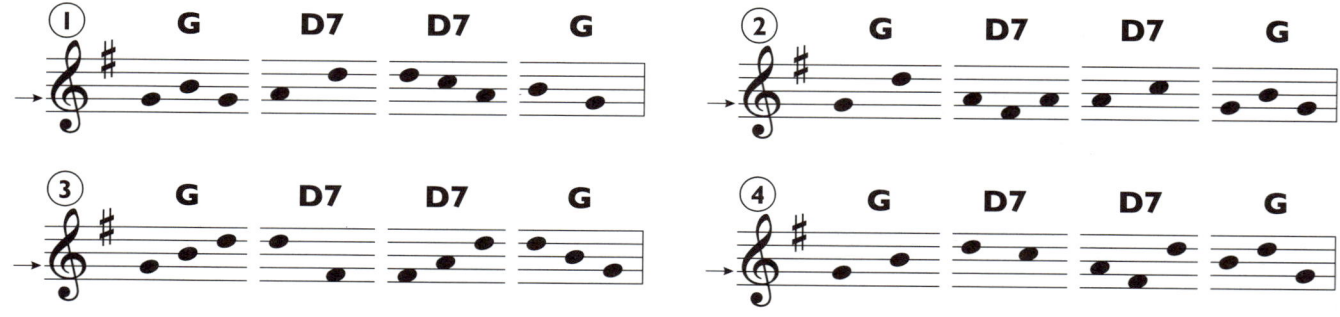

Be expressive when performing with your voice and with your instrument!

TONAL READING
TONIC, DOMINANT, AND SUBDOMINANT FUNCTIONS IN G MAJOR

1. Read the following patterns by singing them WITH TONAL SYLLABLES and by performing them on your instrument. The arrow points to DO. G indicates a TONIC pattern in major tonality; D7 indicates a DOMINANT pattern in major tonality; and C indicates a SUBDOMINANT pattern in major tonality.

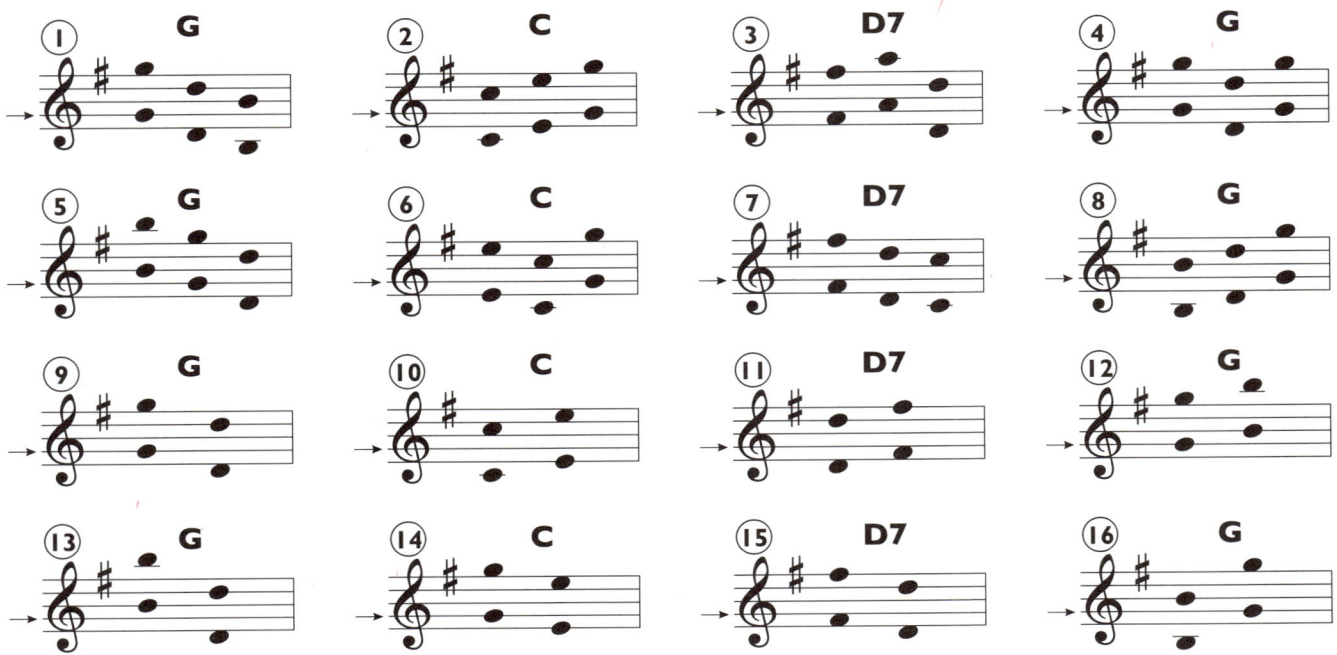

2. Read the following series of patterns by singing them WITH TONAL SYLLABLES and by performing them on your instrument. The arrow points to DO. G indicates a TONIC pattern in major tonality; D7 indicates a DOMINANT pattern in major tonality; and C indicates a SUBDOMINANT pattern in major tonality.

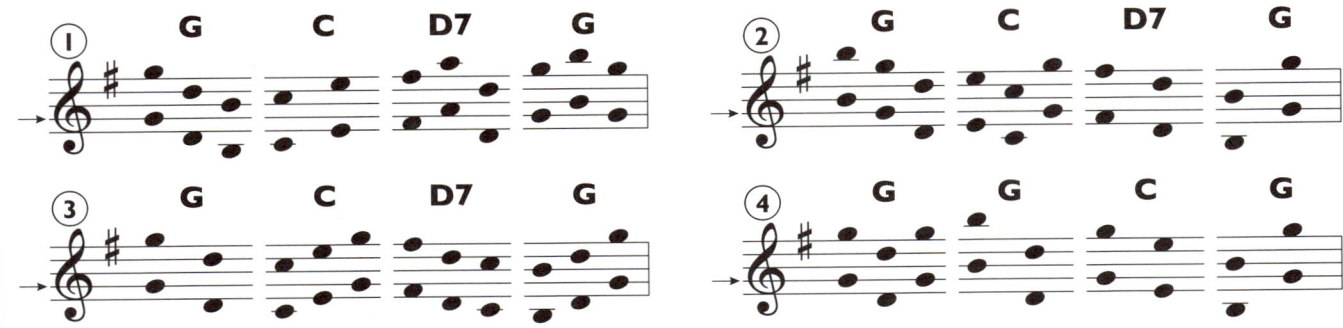

Be expressive when performing with your voice and with your instrument!

GO TELL AUNT RHODY

HOT CROSS BUNS

TWINKLE, TWINKLE, LITTLE STAR

TRIPLE TWINKLE

ENRHYTHMIC READING
MACROBEATS, MICROBEATS, AND DIVISIONS IN DUPLE METER

1. Read the following patterns by chanting them WITH RHYTHM SYLLABLES and by performing them on your instrument. The patterns on the left (4/4) are enrhythmic (they sound the same, but look different) with the patterns on the right (¢).

    The numbers (4, 2) indicate how many macrobeats are in a measure.
    The symbols (♩ , ♪) indicate what kind of a note is a macrobeat.

Be expressive when performing with your voice and with your instrument!

RHYTHM READING
MACROBEATS, MICROBEATS, AND DIVISIONS IN TRIPLE METER

1. Read the following patterns by chanting them WITH RHYTHM SYLLABLES and by performing them on your instrument.

   The number (2) tells how many macrobeats there are in a measure.
   The symbol (♩·) indicates the kind of note that is a macrobeat.

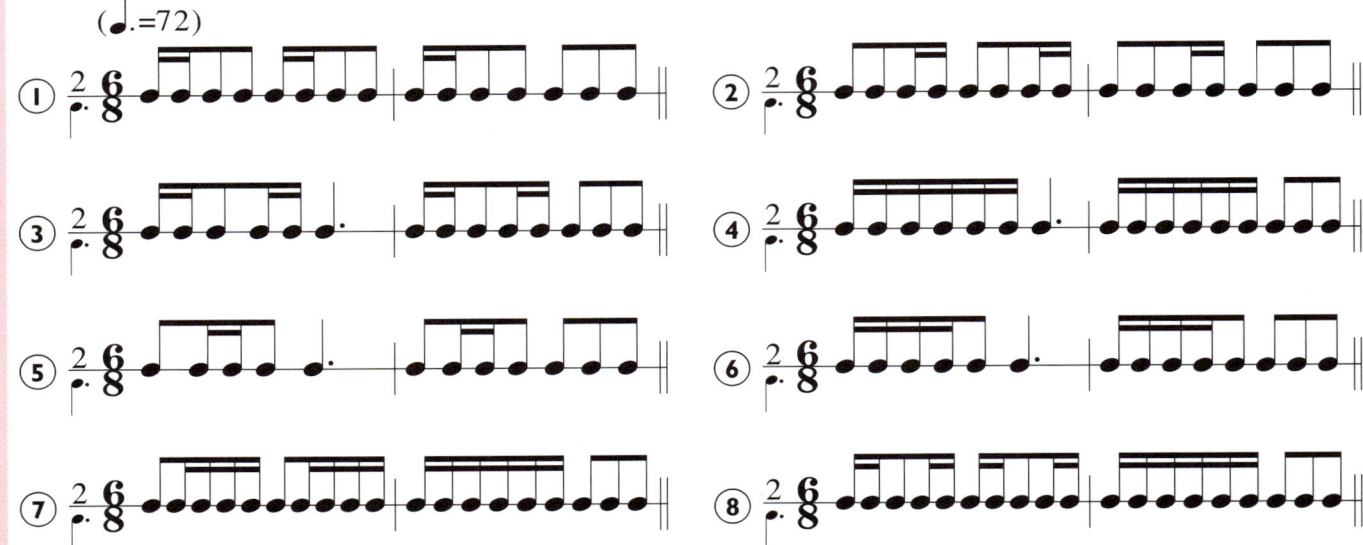

2. Read the following series of patterns by chanting them WITH RHYTHM SYLLABLES and by performing them on your instrument.

   The number (2) tells how many macrobeats there are in a measure.
   The symbol (♩·) indicates the kind of note that is a macrobeat.

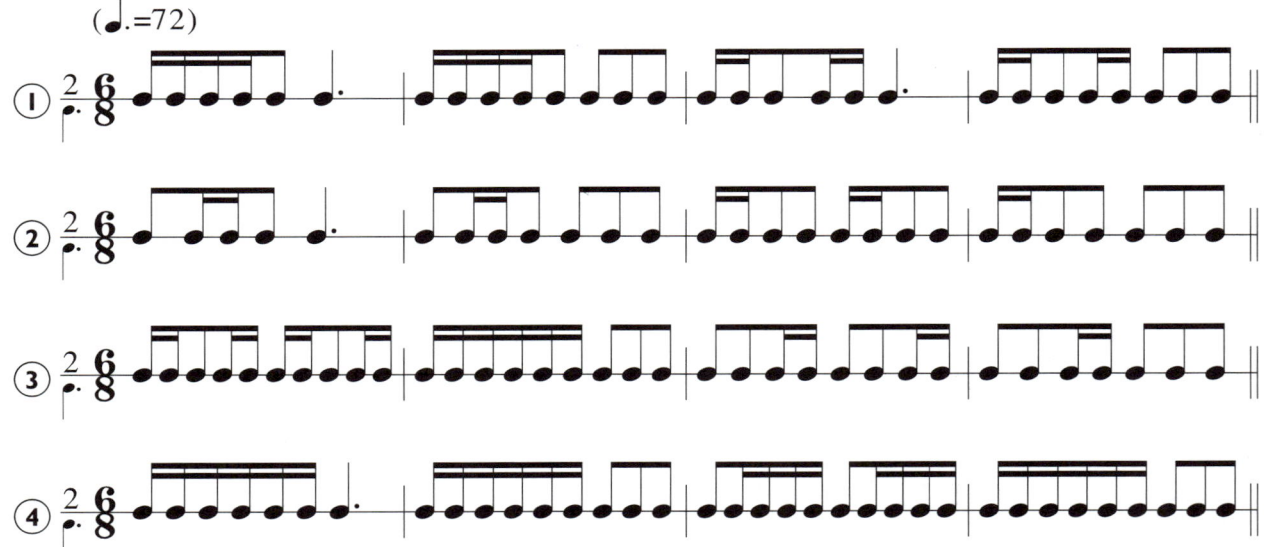

Be expressive when performing with your voice and with your instrument!

ENRHYTHMIC READING
MACROBEATS, MICROBEATS, AND DIVISIONS IN TRIPLE METER

1. Read the following patterns by chanting them WITH RHYTHM SYLLABLES and by performing them on your instrument. The patterns on the left (3/8) are enrhythmic (they sound the same, but look different) with the patterns on the right (3/4).

   The numbers (1, 1) indicate how many macrobeats are in a measure.
   The symbols (♩· , ♩·) indicate what kind of a note is a macrobeat.

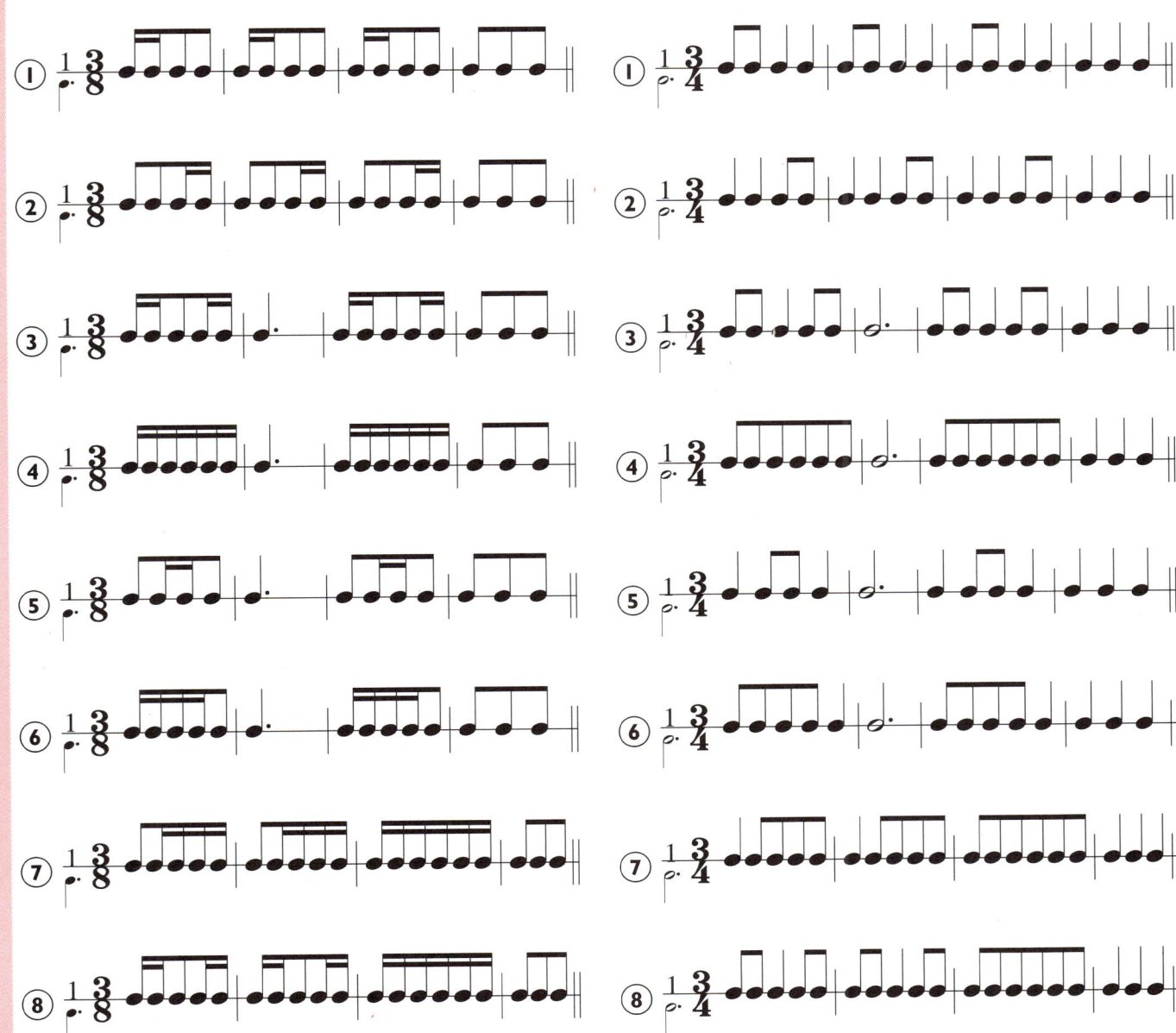

Be expressive when performing with your voice and with your instrument!

DOWN BY THE STATION

MINOR AUNT RHODY

TRIPLE PIERROT

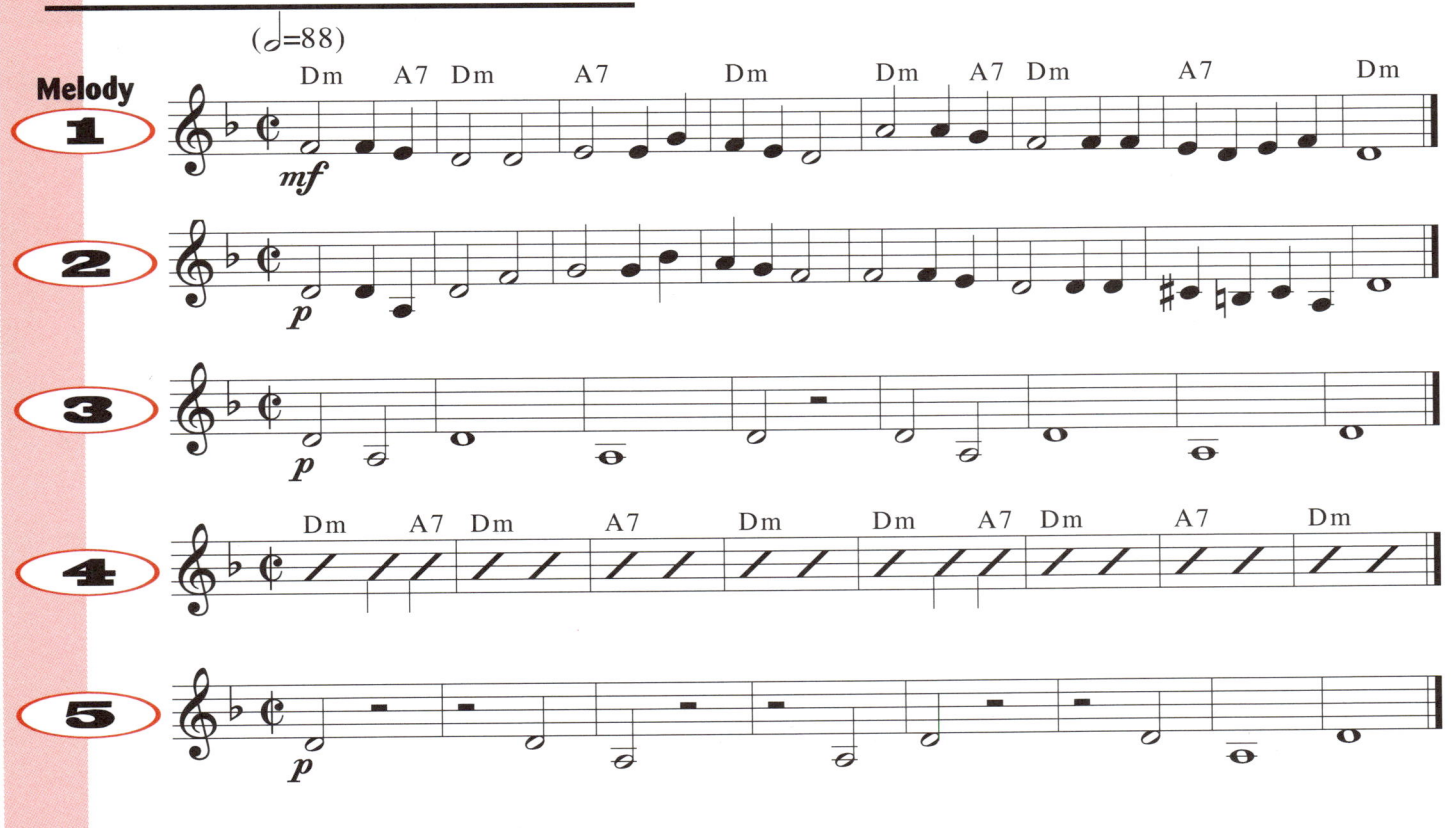

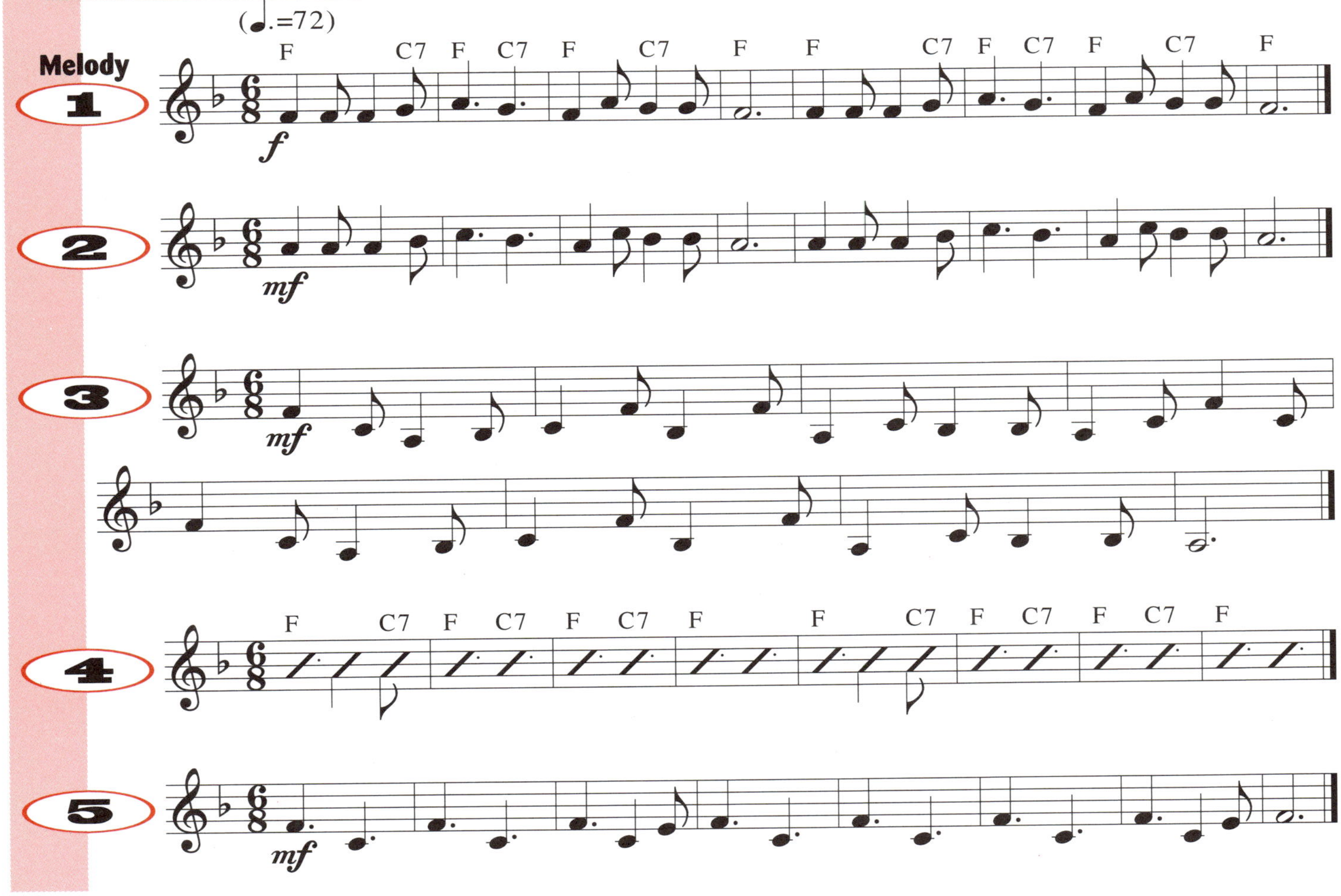

RHYTHM READING
MACROBEATS, MICROBEATS, DIVISIONS, AND ELONGATIONS IN DUPLE METER

1. Read the following patterns by chanting them WITH RHYTHM SYLLABLES and by performing them on your instrument.

   The number (2) tells how many macrobeats there are in a measure.
   The symbol (♩) indicates the kind of note that is a macrobeat.

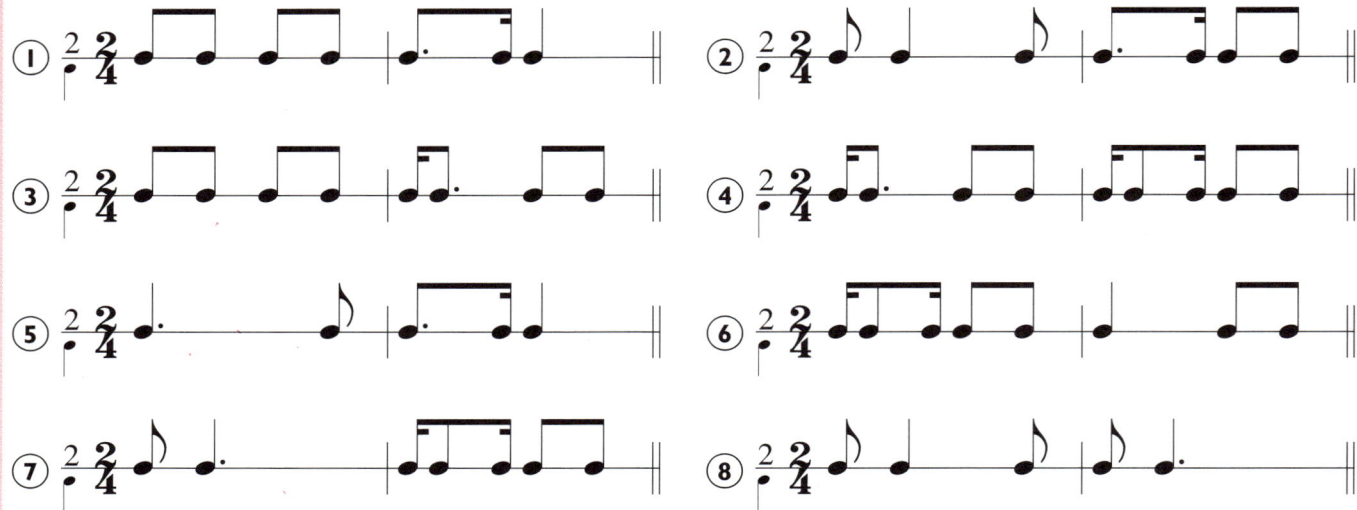

2. Read the following series of patterns by chanting them WITH RHYTHM SYLLABLES and by performing them on your instrument.

   The number (2) tells how many macrobeats there are in a measure.
   The symbol (♩) indicates the kind of note that is a macrobeat.

Be expressive when performing with your voice and with your instrument!

ENRHYTHMIC READING
MACROBEATS, MICROBEATS, DIVISIONS, AND ELONGATIONS IN DUPLE METER

1. Read the following patterns by chanting them WITH RHYTHM SYLLABLES and by performing them on your instrument. The patterns on the left (4/4) are enrhythmic (they sound the same, but look different) with the patterns on the right (¢).

   The numbers (4, 2) indicate how many macrobeats are in a measure.
   The symbols (♩ , ♪) indicate what kind of a note is a macrobeat.

Be expressive when performing with your voice and with your instrument!

LIGHTLY ROW

BAA, BAA, BLACK SHEEP

RHYTHM READING
MACROBEATS, MICROBEATS, DIVISIONS, AND ELONGATIONS IN TRIPLE METER

1. Read the following patterns by chanting them WITH RHYTHM SYLLABLES and by performing them on your instrument.

   The number (2) tells how many macrobeats there are in a measure.
   The symbol (♩·) indicates the kind of note that is a macrobeat.

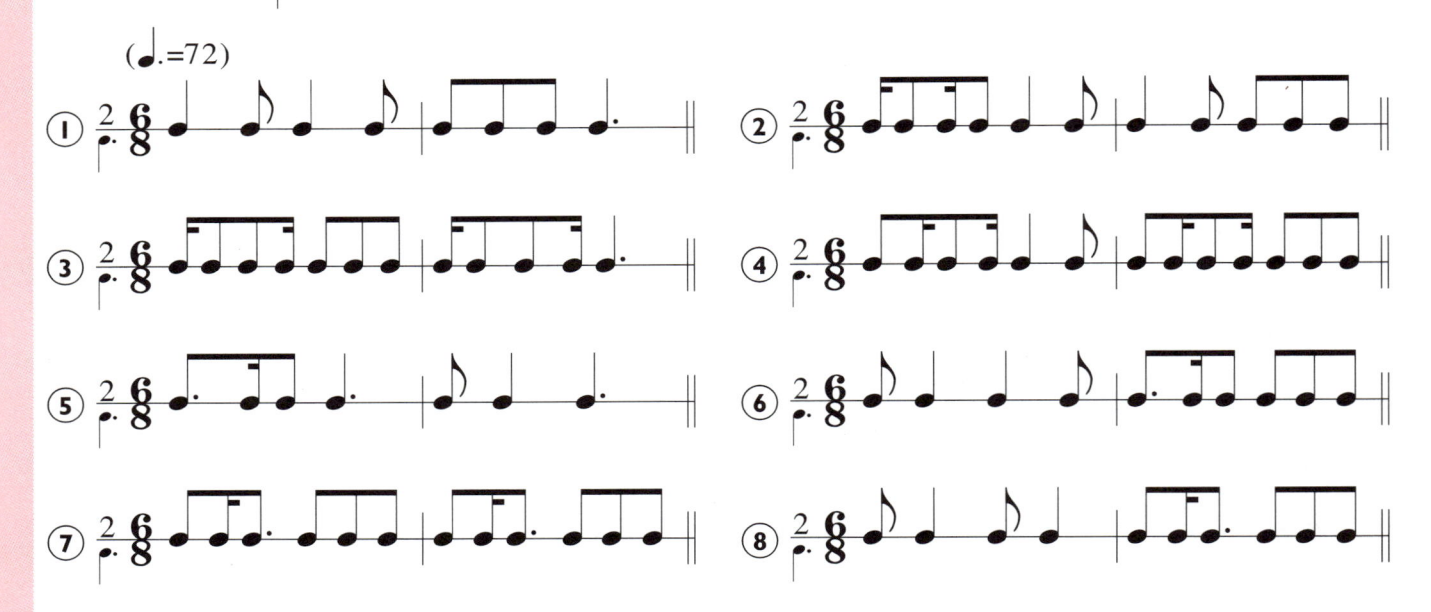

2. Read the following series of patterns by chanting them WITH RHYTHM SYLLABLES and by performing them on your instrument.

   The number (2) tells how many macrobeats there are in a measure.
   The symbol (♩·) indicates the kind of note that is a macrobeat.

Be expressive when performing with your voice and with your instrument!

41

ENRHYTHMIC READING
MACROBEATS, MICROBEATS, DIVISIONS, AND ELONGATIONS IN TRIPLE METER

1. Read the following patterns by chanting them WITH RHYTHM SYLLABLES and by performing them on your instrument. The patterns on the left (3/8) are enrhythmic (they sound the same, but look different) with the patterns on the right (3/4).

   The numbers (1, 1) indicate how many macrobeats are in a measure.
   The symbols (♩· , ♩·) indicate what kind of a note is a macrobeat.

Be expressive when performing with your voice and with your instrument!

PATSY, ORY, ORY, AYE

OATS, PEAS, BEANS

TONAL SIGHT READING

1. Sight read the following patterns by singing them WITH A NEUTRAL SYLLABLE and by performing them on your instrument. Some of the patterns are familiar and some are unfamiliar. The arrow points to DO.

MAJOR
C-DO

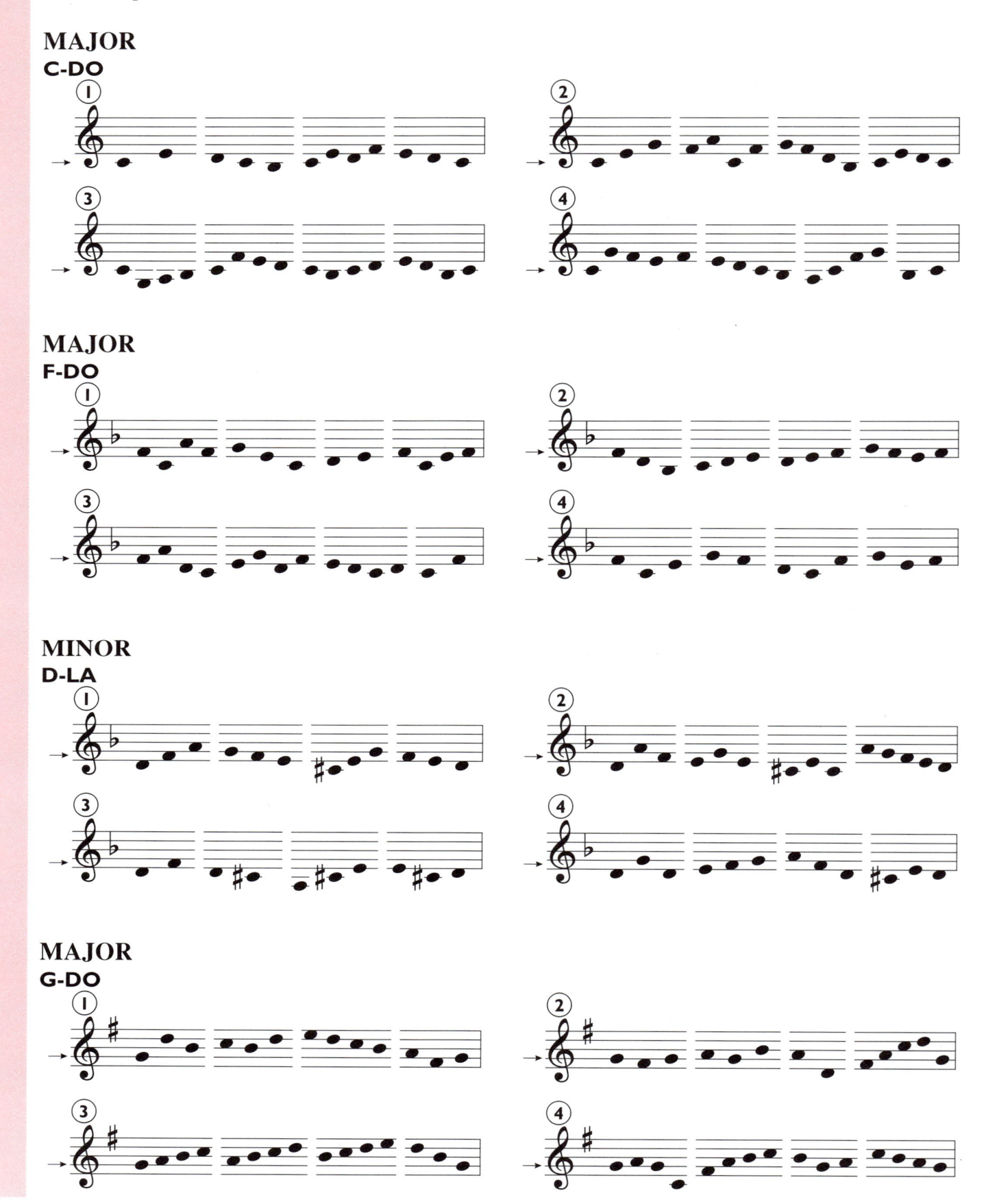

MAJOR
F-DO

MINOR
D-LA

MAJOR
G-DO

RHYTHM SIGHT READING

1. Sight read the following rhythm patterns by chanting them WITH A NEUTRAL SYLLABLE and by performing them on your instrument. Some of the patterns are familiar and some are unfamiliar.

   The number (2) tells how many macrobeats there are in a measure.
   The symbol (♩ or ♩·) indicates the kind of note that is a macrobeat.

DUPLE

TRIPLE

MELODIC SIGHT READING

1. Audiate one of the following melodies. If necessary, SING INDIVIDUAL TONAL PATTERNS WITH TONAL SYLLABLES, and CHANT INDIVIDUAL RHYTHM PATTERNS WITH RHYTHM SYLLABLES. DO NOT SING THE ENTIRE MELODY WITH TONAL SYLLABLES. YOU MAY CHANT THE ENTIRE MELODIC RHYTHM USING RHYTHM SYLLABLES.

2. Audiate that melody while performing it silently on your instrument.

3. Perform that melody on your instrument.

MUSICAL ENRICHMENT

"Musical Enrichment" begins with item #94 on the *Home-Study Compact Disc*. Listen Carefully as a professional musician performs some familiar folk songs. Before each performance the announcer will give the resting tone and starting pitch. For example:

"C is DO, start on DO," indicates that
1) C is the resting tone,
2) the song is in major tonality (because DO is the resting tone), and
3) the song begins on DO.

"D is LA, start on MI," indicates that
1) D is the resting tone,
2) the song is in minor tonality (because LA is the resting tone), and
3) the song begins on MI.

Listen many times to the songs, noting the tone quality, style of articulation, and phrasing. When you can audiate a song (when you can hear it in your head), you may begin to perform that song "by ear." Some of the songs are easy and will require little time to learn to perform. Other songs are more challenging and will require more time to learn to perform. The fingering chart beginning on the next page will help you locate the appropriate DO or LA, and the correct starting pitch. Remember it is alright to make mistakes when you first play "by ear."

Musical Enrichment also includes the activities listed below. Your music teacher will help you mark the charts to indicate when you have satisfactorily completed each of the activities.

A. Sing the song with or without words.
B. Perform the song in the tonality and keyality found on the *Home-Study Compact Disc*.
C. Perform the song in a different keyality. (Start on a different note.)
D. Perform the song with a friend who plays the same or a different instrument.
E. Perform the song in a different meter. (Change from duple to triple or from triple to duple.)
F. Perform the song in a different tonality. (Change from major to minor or from minor to major.)
G. Perform an improvisation or harmony part for the song.

Item/Track No.

1. 94. "Mary Had a Little Lamb" (C is DO; start on MI)
2. 94. "London Bridge" (C is DO; start on SO)
3. 94. "America" (C is DO; start on DO)
4. 95. "Clementine" (F is DO; start on DO)
5. 95. "Hot Cross Buns" (F is DO; start on MI)
6. 95. "Hush Little Baby" (F is DO; start on SO)
7. 96. "Coventry Carol" (D is LA; start on LA)
8. 96. "Snake Dance" (D is LA; start on LA)
9. 96. "This Ol' Hammer" (D is LA; start on LA)
10. 97. "Yankee Doodle" (G is DO; start on DO)
11. 97. "Amazing Grace" (G is DO; start on SO)
12. 97. "Sleep Baby Sleep" (G is DO; start on MI)

CLARINET FINGERINGS

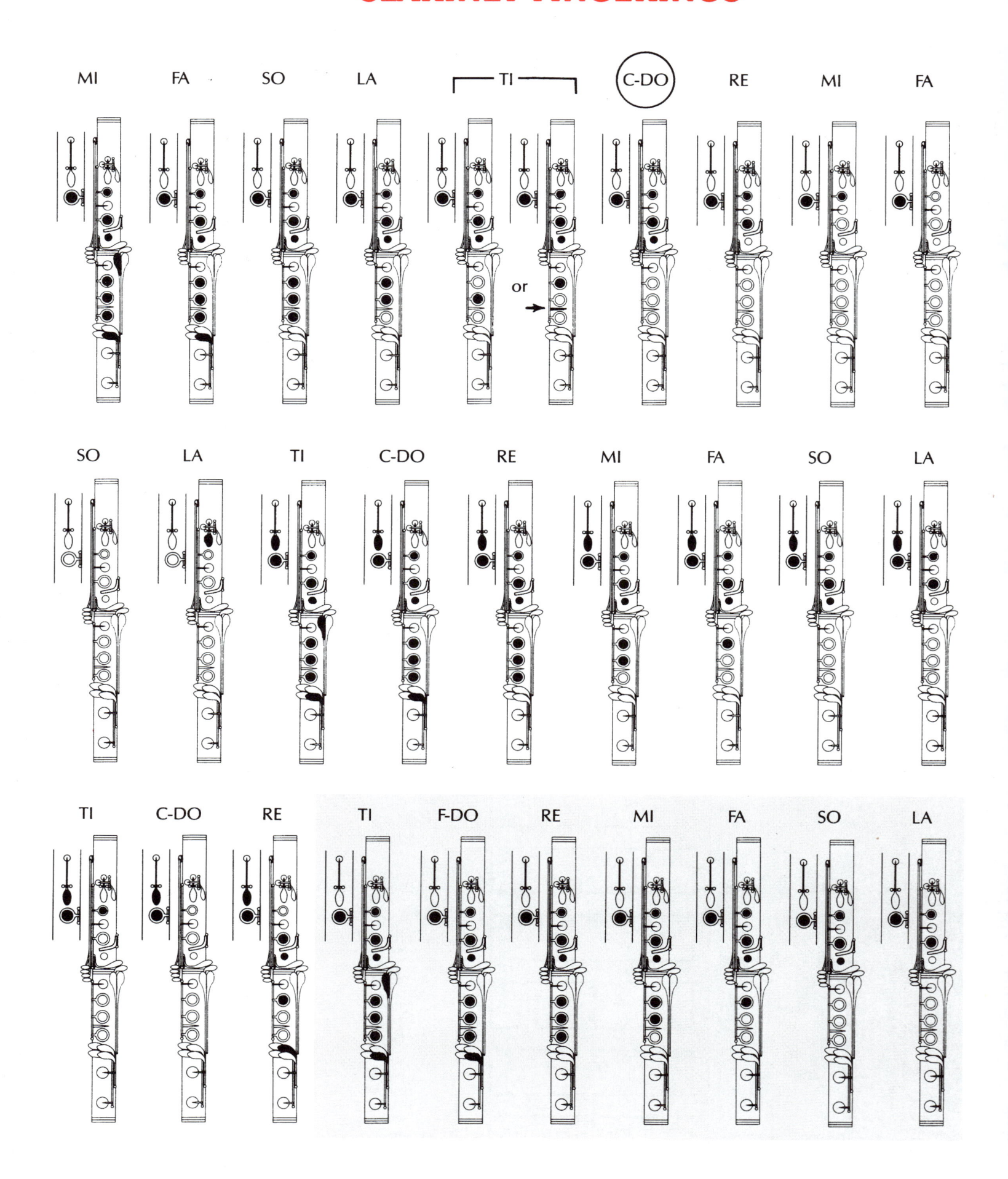